☑ CHECK THE BOXES THAT APPLY TO BEGIN.

☐

I WANT TO DRAW.

☐

I HAVE STORIES TO TELL.

NATHAN HERE!
BY THE END OF THIS
JOURNAL, YOU WILL
LITERALLY LIST 99
STORIES YOU CAN TELL.

I'M SERIOUS.
THE LAST 4 PAGES OF
THE BOOK HAVE 99
BLANKS FOR YOUR
STORY TITLES.

THEY'RE IN YOUR HEAD.
THE JOURNAL WILL
HELP YOU PUT THEM
DOWN IN ONE PLACE.
HERE IS HOW WE'LL
DO IT...

I'LL GIVE YOU DOODLES TO FINISH AND QUESTIONS TO ANSWER, AND AS YOU GO THROUGH EACH ONE, YOUR BRAIN WILL CREATE YOUR

MOST TELLABLE STORIES!

OH YEAHHH! THE ANGRY GOOSE IN THE PARKING LOT!

...AND THEN YOU'LL LIST 99 COMPELLING STORY TITLES!

(ON THE LAST 4 PAGES!)

1. THE DAY I LEARNED TO STEER CLEAR OF GEESE

2.

YOU COULD DO SO MANY THINGS WITH YOUR LIST!

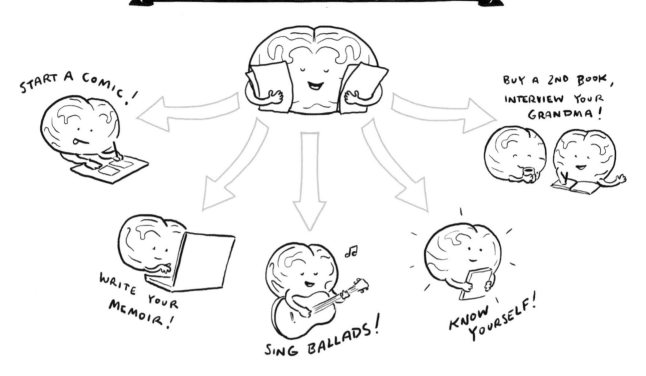

START A COMIC!

BUY A 2ND BOOK, INTERVIEW YOUR GRANDMA!

WRITE YOUR MEMOIR!

SING BALLADS!

KNOW YOURSELF!

THE POSSIBILITIES WILL BE **ENDLESS** ONCE YOU START TO *Narrate Your LIFE!*

EVEN AS YOU READ THIS PAGE, I HOPE YOU START THINKING IN ✦ STORIES ✦

MY LIFE IS ACTUALLY A SERIES OF STORIES!

WAIT — I'M IN A STORY NOW

THINK OF THESE PAGES AS
BUILDING BLOCKS

AT FIRST, YOU'LL PIECE TOGETHER YOUR STORIES SLOWLY AND WILL RELY ON THE DOODLES AND PROMPTS!

BUT AS STORIES COME TO YOU, YOU'LL FIND IT EASIER AND EASIER TO THINK OF THE STORIES ON YOUR OWN.

AND SOON ENOUGH, YOUR BRAIN WON'T NEED HELP AT ALL AND YOU'LL TELL ME TO GO, LIKE IN ONE OF THOSE MOVIES WHERE A WOLF IS RELEASED BACK INTO THE WOODS WHERE IT BELONGS.

UNIQUELY NUMBERED

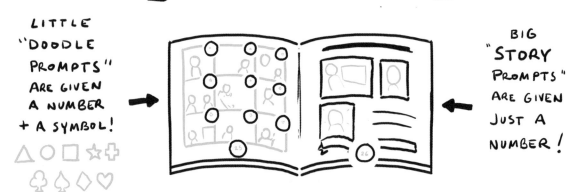

LITTLE
"DOODLE
PROMPTS"
ARE GIVEN
A NUMBER
+ A SYMBOL!

△ ○ □ ☆ ✚
♣ ♠ ◇ ♡

BIG
"STORY
PROMPTS"
ARE GIVEN
JUST A
NUMBER!

this numbering system will

HELP YOU DO THESE 2 THINGS

PIECE TOGETHER PARTS
OF YOUR STORIES

48○ + 48✚

BUY THIS!

OK

I REGRET
BUYING THAT

(THAT TIME MY BFF CONVINCED
ME TO BUY THE <u>WORST</u> SHIRT)

PROVIDE VISUAL AIDS
TO YOUR STORY LIST

*next to each story
title, list a prompt #*

STORY TITLE	PROMPT #
1. THE DAY I LEARNED TO STEER CLEAR OF GEESE	94
2. MY WORST PURCHASE EVER (BECKY!!!)	48○ + 48✚
3.	
4.	
5.	

LET'S START DRAWING!

 DRAW OVER THE LINES!

 DRAW AROUND THE LINES!

 USE THE LINES AS YOU WISH!

 MAKE LITTLE CHANGES!

 LITTLE CHANGES CAN DO A LOT!

 OR MAKE BIG CHANGES!

 NOW YOU TRY!

TRY DRAWING THESE FACES!

NOW DRAW YOUR OWN FACE!

DO IT AGAIN!

PRACTICE DRAWING YOUR OWN FACIAL EXPRESSIONS

NOW
DO
IT
BIG!

Miscellaneous

Drawing Tips

ADD **WORDS** AND **SYMBOLS** OVERHEAD TO CONVEY EMOTIONS!

THE CHARACTERS WITH WIDER MOUTHS & EYES ARE MEANT TO BE `KIDS`

(16)

WHEN FILLING BANNERS... COUNT YOUR LETTERS

(15)

SO THAT YOU CAN... SPACE THEM EVENLY

Practice Pages

WRARR ZZZZT

IF YOU EVER DRAW SOMETHING POORLY MAKE THE THING INTRODUCE ITSELF.

Hi! I'm a cup of coffee

SOMETHING COMPLETELY WRONG
I BELIEVED AS A KID

A VISUAL REPRESENTATION OF WHAT I BELIEVED

HOW I WOULD EXPLAIN IT

DRAW YOUR KID SELF

DRAW YOUR KID SELF

HOW I FELT REALIZIN' THE TRUTH

DRAW YOURSELF REALIZIN'

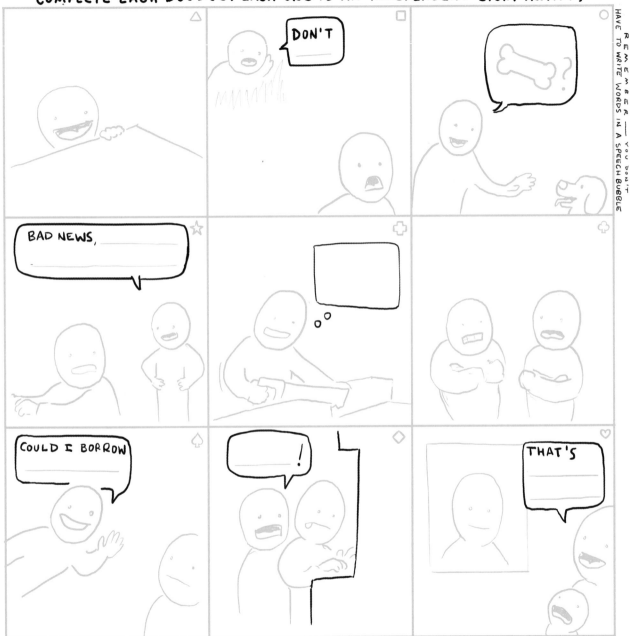

1 SOMETHING MY FRIENDS LOVE THAT I DON'T CARE FOR

DRAW YOURSELF, THE THING, AND YOUR *WRONG* FRIENDS

2 SOMETHING I LOVE THAT MY FRIENDS DON'T CARE FOR

DRAW YOUR *WRONG* FRIENDS, THE THING, AND YOU

WHY MY FRIENDS ARE <u>WRONG</u>

1

2

5 THINGS THAT OFFEND my senses

DRAW YOURSELF AND EACH OFFENDING THING

SOUND

SIGHT

FEEL

TASTE

SMELL

THE WORST OF THESE IS...

please explain:

DRAW THE SHOW'S TITLE SCREEN

REASON FOR THIS RULE

MY REACTION TO THIS RULE

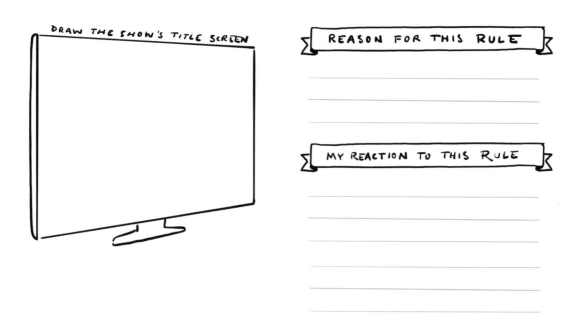

CHECK ONE OF THE BOXES AND DRAW YOURSELF IN THE BOX THAT APPLIES.

I SNUCK IT

I DID NOT

8

CHARACTER NAME:

FICTIONAL CHARACTER THAT GAVE ME NIGHTMARES

DRAW YOU + THE CHARACTER

CHOOSE THE SOURCE.
DRAW THE DETAILS:

DRAW YOURSELF

- A SIX-WORD SUMMARY OF -
WHY THEY WERE SO SCARY

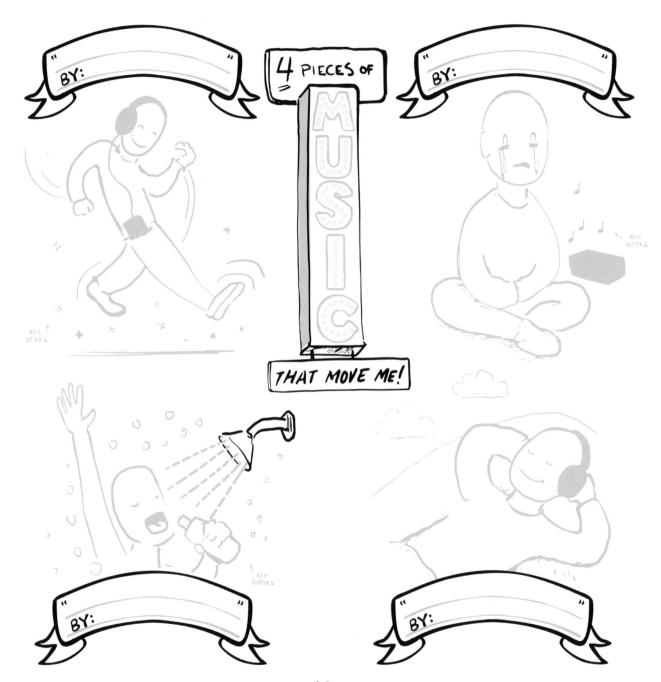

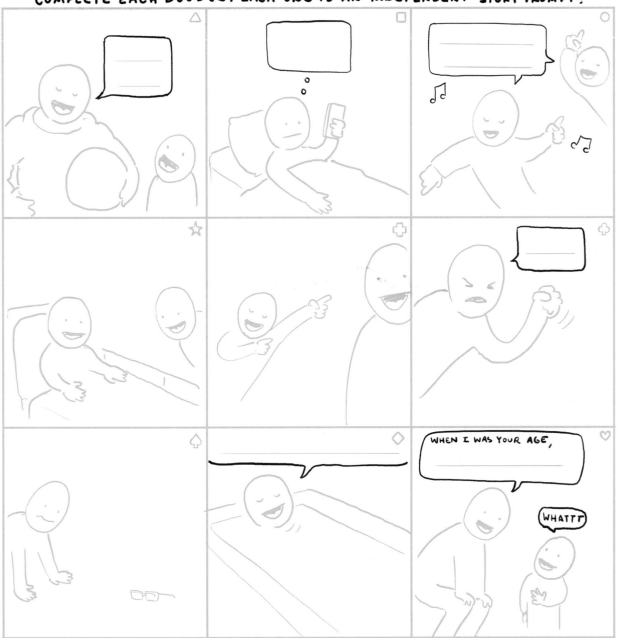

MY CLOSEST BRUSH WITH A STAR I ADMIRE

WHERE WERE YOU?

_____

IT WAS NONE OTHER THAN...

← THEM

ME ↓

DRAW YOURSELF AND YOUR THOUGHTS.

DESCRIBE THE MOMENT:

_____

_____

_____

CHECK ONE OF THE BOXES AND DRAW YOURSELF.

KEPT MY COOL

LOST MY COOL

DRAW YOUR
EXCITED SELF

LIFE EVENT THAT LIVED UP TO MY

HIGH EXPECTATIONS

DRAW YOUR
ELATED SELF

WHAT I EXPECTED!

_____
_____
_____
_____
_____
_____
_____
_____
_____
_____
_____

HOW IT TURNED OUT!

_____
_____
_____
_____
_____
_____
_____
_____
_____
_____
_____

LESSON LEARNED

DRAW YOURSELF
CELEBRATIN'

FIVE UNFORGETTABLE HORIZONS

draw the memorable views you have seen

WHAT WAS YOUR FACIAL EXPRESSION?

WHAT DID THE HORIZON LOOK LIKE?

CLOSE YOUR EYES AND THINK BACK ON THESE VIEWS. WHICH ONE CALMS YOU MOST? AND WHY?

18

SOMETHING I LOVED AS A KID THAT I NO LONGER LOVE

what changed in you?

YOU THEN

YOU NOW

SOMETHING I LOVED AS A KID THAT I STILL LOVE NOW

what stayed the same?

YOU THEN

YOU NOW

DRAW THE MOVIE SCREEN

DRAW THE MOVIE SCREEN

DRAW YOUR YOUNG SELF

character name:
_____

MEMORABLE CHILDHOOD CINEMA EXPERIENCE

MOVIE
TITLE: _____

WHY I RECALL IT VIVIDLY

MOVIE CHARACTER I RELATE TO

MOVIE
TITLE: _____

WHY I CONNECT W/ THEM

DRAW YOURSELF DOING THE ACTIVITIES BELOW AND RANK IN ORDER OF PREFERENCE (1=MOST; 3=LEAST)

MY WORST MEMORY IN THE RAIN

25 + 26

A TALE OF ANCIENT TECHNOLOGY
I WILL AMAZE FUTURE GENERATIONS WITH

WHEN I WAS YOUNGER

DRAW YOUR FUTURE SELF TALKING TO SPACE BABIES.

how many of these do you recall?

FILL IN THE LINES AND ADD DETAILS

WHEN I WAS YOUNGER...

28

style HIGHLIGHTS OF MY YOUTH

DRAW THEM
ON YOUR
YOUNG SELF
↳

essential items

_____
_____
_____
_____

essential items

_____
_____
_____
_____

essential items

_____
_____
_____
_____

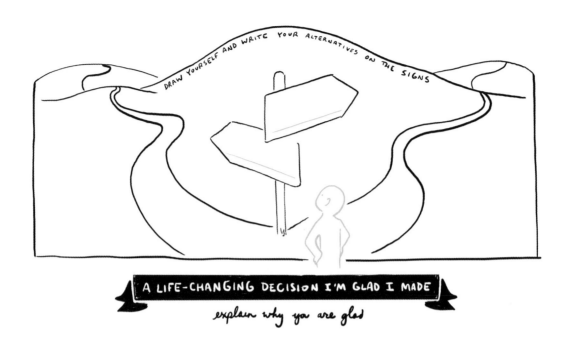

DRAW YOURSELF AND WRITE YOUR ALTERNATIVES ON THE SIGNS

A LIFE-CHANGING DECISION I'M GLAD I MADE

explain why you are glad

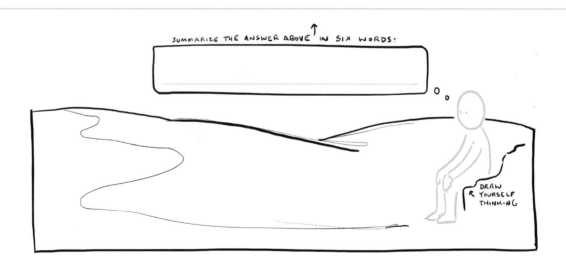

SUMMARIZE THE ANSWER ABOVE IN SIX WORDS:

DRAW YOURSELF THINKING

NAME IT

DRAW IT

DRAW YOU

A TIME I LOVED THIS FOOD A BIT TOO MUCH

draw the cover ↱

A BOOK THAT BLEW MY MIND

WHY IT STUCK WITH ME:

MY 5 MAIN HAIR PHASES

DRAW YOUR HAIR AND NAME THE PHASE.

_____ _____ _____ _____ _____

MY MOST REGRETTABLE HAIR PHASE:

_____

_____

_____

_____

IN MY DEFENSE:

_____

———————————— *practice here* ————————————

BALLET DANCER

38

A FAMILY QUOTE THAT STILL MAKES US LAUGH

DRAW YOURSELVES LAUGHING. DRAW OTHERS IN!

THE BACKSTORY, AS BEST I CAN TELL IT:

the FRIEND I CAN BE MY WEIRDEST SELF WITH

COMPLETE THE DRAWING

A TALE OF PEAK WEIRDNESS

_____

_____

_____

_____

_____

_____

* SEE BACK OF THIS PAGE

A NEAR-DEATH EXPERIENCE

I was...

When suddenly...

* (choose one)

☐ I almost died!

☐ I could have died.

☐ It was super dangerous.

☐ I was scared.

☐ _____

when I think back on this, I remember...

DRAW YOUR MEMORY

DRAW YOURSELF

44

ADD COSTUME ↓

MY BEST CHILDHOOD HALLOWEEN COSTUME

costume description

_____

_____

_____

_____

DRAW THE MOST ESSENTIAL ITEM:

HOW IT WOULD LOOK IF **SOMEONE WENT AS ME FOR HALLOWEEN**

costume description

DRAW THE MOST ESSENTIAL ITEM:

_____

_____

_____

_____

ADD COSTUME ↓

46 + 47

why we get along

why we fight*

* WHAT THEY ARE WRONG ABOUT

DRAW YOU TWO

49·50

CHARACTER'S NAME. USE BIG LETTERS!

DRAW YOUR REACTION AND THEIR DEATH SCENE.

DRAW YOUR EXPRESSION

MY EMOTION

NAME EMOTION

DRAW THE CHARACTER

R.I.P.

CHARACTER'S NAME

HOW THEY DIED

WHY I REMEMBER IT VIVIDLY

A SIX-WORD EULOGY

52

a **Mountain** [THAT I CLIMBED!*]

*METAPHORICALLY SPEAKING UNLESS YOU DID CLIMB A LITERAL MOUNTAIN AND YOU WOULD RATHER DISCUSS THAT

MOUNTAIN NAME:

DRAW YOUR PRE-CLIMB SELF
AND YOUR PRE-CLIMB THOUGHTS

...HOW I CONQUERED IT

ONE SUCCINCT PIECE OF ADVICE I WOULD SHOUT DOWN TO MY PRE-CLIMB SELF IF I COULD.

FILL IN LETTERS

LIKE THIS

ME AS A ROBOT

CUSTOMIZE THIS ROBOT AS YOU SEE FIT.

NAME THE ROBOT:

56

DRAW OR WRITE YOUR LIST!

TOUCH

SMELL

SIGHT

SOUND

TASTE

Sensory Experiences

THAT RECHARGE MY BATTERY

THE MOST SURPRISING ITEM ON
THIS LIST AND HOW I FOUND IT

Someone who

CHANGED THE COURSE OF MY LIFE

NAME:

BEFORE WE MET,
_____
_____
_____
_____
_____

BUT THEN MY LIFE TOOK A TURN!

WE FIRST MET WHEN
_____
_____
_____
_____
_____

HERE IS HOW MY LIFE CHANGED:
_____
_____
_____
_____
_____
_____
_____

HOW I USED TO THINK

DRAW YOURSELF THINKIN'

DRAW THE MOMENT YOU MET

HOW I THINK NOW

DRAW YOURSELF THINKIN' NEW THINKS

TRY DRAWING THESE FACES AGAIN!

(TURN BACK TO THE BEGINNING TO SEE YOUR PROGRESS.)

NOW DRAW YOUR OWN FACE!

DO IT AGAIN!

PRACTICE DRAWING YOUR OWN FACIAL EXPRESSIONS

NOW
DO
IT
BIG!

DRAW YOUR EXPRESSION

DRAW STIMULI

WRITE EMOTION HERE

HAPPY

DRAW ONE FACE EACH DAY FOR TWELVE DAYS

66

A FEW OF MY QUESTIONABLE CHOICES

OVERALL LOOK

DRAW IT ↙

HAIR

← DRAW IT ↗

ACCESSORIES

A NOTABLE STYLE OBSSESSION:

IN MY DEFENSE...

68

FOUR MOVIE SCENES THAT GIVE ME FEELINGS

DRAW THE CLIMACTIC MOMENT IN THE SCENE AND YOUR FACE

MOVIE TITLE

MOVIE TITLE

MY FAVORITE SAD MOVIE IS...

"_____"

PROBABLY BECAUSE _____

MY FAVORITE FUNNY MOVIE IS...

"_____"

PROBABLY BECAUSE _____

MOVIE TITLE

MOVIE TITLE

70 + 71

DRAW YOUR
HAPPY / SAD SELF →

CHART THE EMOTIONAL FLOW OF A TYPICAL WEEK. MARK THE HIGH/LOW.

HAPPY THINGS

SAD THINGS

M   T   W   T   F   S   S

COFFEE

ADD △ (THE HIGH POINT), ADD ▽ (THE LOW POINT), ADD 🥤 🥣 OATMEAL 🍦 (CRUCIAL FOOD/DRINKS)

HERE ARE THE HABITS THAT HELP ME TO...

SUSTAIN THE HIGHS

MITIGATE THE LOWS

73+74

MY FIRST PAYCHECK

A.K.A. THAT TIME THEY PAID ME TO BE A:

← DRAW YOURSELF IN YOUR WORK OUTFIT

MY MAIN RESPONSIBILITIES:

-
-
-
-

GIVE YOUR ADVICE TO ANYONE STARTING THIS JOB. DRAW AND WRITE:

1
2

1
2

#1 DO:

#2 DO:

#1 DON'T:

#2 DON'T:

76

 MY REACTIONS TO SOME COMMON PHOBIAS

DRAW YOURSELF REACTING →

SPIDERS
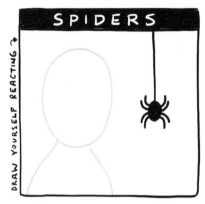

DEEP WATER
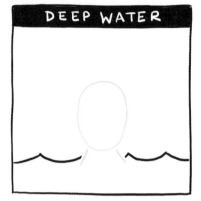

THE DARK

PUBLIC SPEAKING

HEIGHTS

CLOWNS

THE THING THAT SCARES ME MOST IS:

THE REASON I'M AFRAID IS ONE TIME...

78

DRAW YOUR NOW-SELF ↑ AND YOUR KID-SELF.

IF I COULD TELL MY KID SELF ONE STORY

WHAT I HOPE
THIS WOULD
ACCOMPLISH :

9 INFLUENTIAL FRIENDS

EXPANDS MY
CULINARY WORLD

NAME ↗

CONVINCES ME
TO TRAVEL

SPARKS MY
PHOTOGRAPHIC EYE

AWAKENS MY
ARTISTIC SIDE

HELPS ME
NOTICE NATURE

TEACHES ME TO
BE PATIENT

INSPIRES ME TO
READ MORE

GETS ME MOVING

THE STORY OF A PERMANENT CHANGE IN ME SPARKED BY A FRIEND

AN EXPERIENCE THAT LED TO A PERSONAL TRANSFORMATION

DRAW DETAILS!

THE EXPERIENCE

AFTER, I WAS

BEFORE, I WAS

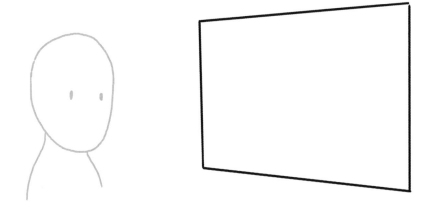

FAMOUS EVENT I WATCHED ON LIVE TV

DRAW THE TV AND **YOUR** REACTION TO IT

THE DATE

MY LOCATION

LIFE EVENT THAT DID NOT LIVE UP TO MY

HIGH EXPECTATIONS

THE EVENT

HOW IT TURNED OUT...

WHAT I EXPECTED!

LESSON LEARNED

⭐ CONCENTRATING

⭐ DRIVING IN AN UNFAMILIAR PLACE!

⭐ MEETING A DOG!

⭐ WAKING UP!

⭐ SAYING GOODBYE!

⭐ HOLDING A BABY!

FILL IN ONE ⭐
DESCRIBE A MOMENT
YOU MADE THIS FACE. GIVE
THE STORY A SHORT TITLE.

DRAW A SCENE FROM
THE NEWS COVERAGE OF THE EVENT

A SOUND FROM THE TV:

EARTHQUAKE   HURRICANE   WILDFIRE   TORNADO   TSUNAMI

VOLCANIC   LANDSLIDE   LIGHTNING   FLOOD
ERUPTION   STRIKE

THE MOMENT OF HIGHEST ANXIETY WAS:

MOST VIVID SENSORY
M E M O R Y

WHO WAS WITH ME:
DRAW THEIR RESPECTIVE EMOTIONS

NAMES: _____ _____ _____ _____

my worst encounter

my best encounter

_____

_____

_____

_____

_____

_____

_____

_____

_____

_____

_____

_____

_____

_____

CHOOSE ONE

BEACH   CITY   MOUNTAINS

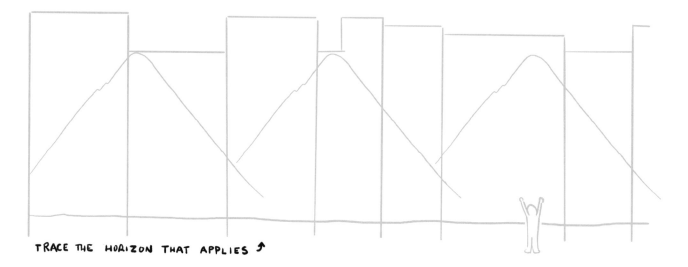

TRACE THE HORIZON THAT APPLIES ↑

DRAW YOURSELF IN
THE EXPERIENCE

97

FOUR PHOTOS — I'M PROUD OF

LOOK AT THE PHOTOS — THEN DRAW THE PHOTOS!

CHOOSE 1

TELL THE BACKSTORY

99

:99 STORIES I COULD TELL:

WRITE A COMPELLING STORY TITLE HERE ↴

WRITE THE PROMPT # HERE
(E.G. 27♡ OR 54)↴

1		
2		
3		
4		
5		
6		
7		
8		
9		
10		
11		
12		
13		
14		
15		
16		
17		
18		
19		
20		
21		
22		
23		
24		

	STORY TITLE	PROMPT #
25		
26		
27		
28		
29		
30		
31		
32		
33		
34		
35		
36		
37		
38		
39		
40		
41		
42		
43		
44		
45		
46		
47		
48		
49		

	STORY TITLE	PROMPT #
50		
51		
52		
53		
54		
55		
56		
57		
58		
59		
60		
61		
62		
63		
64		
65		
66		
67		
68		
69		
70		
71		
72		
73		
74		

	STORY TITLE	PROMPT #
75		
76		
77		
78		
79		
80		
81		
82		
83		
84		
85		
86		
87		
88		
89		
90		
91		
92		
93		
94		
95		
96		
97		
98		
99		

MORROW
GIFT

AN IMPRINT OF WILLIAM MORROW

HarperCollins books may be purchased for educational, business, or sales promotional use. For information, please email the Special Markets Dept. at SPsales@harpercollins.com

Designed by Nathan W. Pyle
    Library of Congress Cataloging-in-Publication Data has been applied for.
ISBN 978-0-06-274835-5

20 21 22 23 IM   10 9 8 7 6 5 4 3 2